auto racing's
new wave

Dale
Earnhardt Jr.

Driven by Destiny

BY
MARK STEWART

THE MILLBROOK PRESS
BROOKFIELD, CONNECTICUT

M

THE MILLBROOK PRESS

Produced by
BITTERSWEET PUBLISHING
John Sammis, President
and
TEAM STEWART, INC.
RESEARCHED AND EDITED BY MIKE KENNEDY

Series Design and Electronic Page Makeup by
JAFFE ENTERPRISES
Ron Jaffe

All photos courtesy AP/ Wide World Photos, Inc., except the following:
© Brian Spurlock, SportsChrome USA — Cover
The following images are from the collection of Team Stewart:
Biscoe Collection — Page 6
The Upper Deck Company © 1999 — Page 21
Ford Motor Company © 2000 — Page 31
Primedia © 2000 — Page 32
The Upper Deck Company © 2000 — Page 36 bottom
Sports Illustrated/Time Inc. © 2001 — Page 39

Printed in the United States of America

Published by
The Millbrook Press, Inc.
2 Old New Milford Road
Brookfield, Connecticut   06804
www.millbrookpress.com

Library of Congress Cataloging-in-Publication Data

Stewart, Mark.
   Dale Earnhardt Jr. : driven by destiny / by Mark Stewart.
      p. cm. — (Auto racing's new wave)
   Includes index.
   Summary: A biography of the NASCAR driver who is the son
of another winning racecar driver, Dale Earnhardt, Sr.
   ISBN 0-7613-2908-0 (lib. bdg.)
   1. Earnhardt, Dale, Jr.—Juvenile literature. 2. Automobile
racing drivers—United States—Biography—Juvenile literature.
   [1. Earnhardt, Dale, Jr. 2. Automobile racing drivers.]   I.
Title. II. Series.
   GV1032.E19S74 2003
   796.72'092—dc21
   [B]
                                                    2002014113

1 3 5 7 9 10 8 6 4 2

Contents

Family Business

chapter

> *"My father and grandfather have made a good name for my family."*
> — DALE EARNHARDT JR.

In the early days of stock-car racing, long before today's superspeedways came to be, the field of battle was the dirt track. Drivers pushed cars built to go 60 miles (96.5 km) per hour to speeds over 100 mph (161 kph), on tiny ovals made of banked earth. Every lap was a kind of controlled spinout. There were no seat belts or fire suits, and the guardrails ringing the track were there for show more than anything. In this era of racing, one man stood above all others. His name was Ralph Earnhardt.

Ralph could take a vehicle that had been all "raced out" and work miracles with it. He was a magician when it came to building cars, and because he knew every rut and

Dale Earnhardt Jr. makes a good living from his many endorsements. He knows none of this would be possible without the hard work and sacrifice of stock-car racing's pioneers, including his grandfather, Ralph Earnhardt.

Postcards of Ralph Earnhardt are still popular among racing fans, especially those who root for his grandson.

bump on every track in the country, he could set up his cars perfectly for each event. When the green flag came down and the drivers roared away, Ralph drove with a rare mix of intelligence and daring. He sensed when to hang back and when to surge forward. He could take a lead early and hold it, or bide his time and win in the final stages.

Did You Know?

Dale Jr.'s name is actually Ralph Earnhardt III. Dale is his middle name. Dale Sr.'s name was actually Ralph Earnhardt Jr. His middle name was Dale, too.

Either way, he usually won—sometimes three or four races a week.

Ralph Earnhardt was a legend in late-model racing during the 1950s and 1960s. He was still going strong in the early 1970s, when he was in his forties. By that time his son, Dale, was making his own way on the stock-car circuit. The two had butted heads for many years when Dale was a teenager; Ralph had always hoped his boy would get a "regular" job,

Dale Earnhardt Sr. (car #2) was one of stock car racing's top competitors from the 1970s on.

but Dale didn't feel right unless he was up to his elbows in a racing engine. When Dale quit school in the ninth grade to work on cars, his father saw that he would not be deterred and brought him into the family business. In 1972, the two actually entered the same race together. But Dale had his sights set higher, on the Winston Cup circuit. He eventually left dirt-track competition to race on asphalt. A few months later, in September 1973, Ralph died from heart failure.

Dale inherited from his father a single-mindedness that would make him a great driver. This focus also steadied him through some lean years, when he barely made enough to feed his family. Unfortunately, it also made Dale a hard man to live with. When Ralph passed away, Dale had already been married and divorced, and he had a son, Kerry. He remarried a woman named Brenda, and they had a daughter, Kelley. They had a second child on October 10, 1974, and named him Dale Jr.

The oldest Earnhardt boy, Kerry, followed in his dad's footsteps.

Father Knows Best

chapter 1

"I'd just as soon he be a doctor."
— DALE EARNHARDT SR.

ale Earnhardt's second marriage did not work out, and three years later Brenda left and took her two children. In 1979, a fire swept through their house, leaving them homeless. The kids moved in with their father in Mooresville, North Carolina, while their mother got back on her feet. Dale Sr. was just starting to make decent money as a Winston Cup driver, but spent almost all of his time on the road. Kelley and Dale Jr. almost never saw their father, who hired a nanny to take care of them. Mostly they just talked to him on the phone.

"He's a terrific young man, if I do say so myself."
BRENDA JACKSON, DALE JR.'S MOM

Dale Sr. attends a NASCAR banquet with his third wife, Teresa. Dale Jr. had a hard time adjusting after his parents were divorced.

When Dale Jr. and Dale Sr. did get to spend time together, they concentrated on going fast and having fun. That was how Ralph had raised his boy, and Dale Sr. aimed to do things the same way. When Dale Jr. was six, his dad took him water skiing—the Earnhardt way. He tied a rope onto the back of a pickup truck and threw the other end to his son, who was waiting in the water. Then Dale Sr. gunned it and tore down a dirt road. The day ended when Dale Jr. hit a boathouse. Luckily, he was not seriously injured.

Dale Sr. married for the third time in 1982, to Teresa Houston. She accompanied her husband on the road, so the kids continued to be raised by nannies. This was a difficult time for Dale Jr., who really needed a man around the house. "He was smaller than other people in his grade, and he was shy," confirms his sister, Kelley. "People always walked over him and didn't treat him with respect. I was the one Dale Jr. came to when he needed to talk."

Dale Jr. got his start in go-karts. He still loves to race them.

Dale Sr. is helped off the track by a fellow driver after a 1982 wreck. Scenes like these frightened Dale Jr., but did not keep him from getting into the sport.

By junior high, Dale Jr. was starting to rebel. He ignored his chores, talked back to his teachers, and did anything to get his father's attention. When he was expelled from school in seventh grade, Dale Sr. had had enough. He shipped Dale Jr. to the Oak Ridge Military Academy in Oak Ridge, North Carolina. Although the thought of military school was appalling to Dale Jr. at the time, looking back he believes the experience benefited him greatly. "I will always believe that I was 10 times the person after that," Dale Jr. maintains. "It made me smarter, stronger, and less likely to get my butt kicked."

With Dale Sr. less worried about his boy's discipline problems, the two were able to relax and enjoy each other's company. Dale Jr.'s competitive streak was starting to emerge, and his dad got a huge kick out of watching him race go-karts with his friends. Once Dale Sr. hopped on a Honda ATV and took off after the teenagers, just to see

Dale Sr. waves to the crowd after winning the 1986 Busch Classic. He was at the peak of his career when Dale Jr. was in high school.

what they would do when they realized NASCAR's famous "Intimidator" was on their tails. Dale Jr. remembers it differently. He thinks his father could not stand watching a race without trying to win it!

Dale Jr. left Oak Ridge after two years and came back home to attend Mooresville Senior High School. His dad was in the prime of his career, probably the most recognizable athlete in the state. This did not make his son a popular student, however. His teachers and classmates recall that Dale Jr. had a small, tight group of friends and that he became closer to his older half brother, Kerry, during this time. Their common interest was racing. Kerry was just getting into the sport, and the two boys spent hours in the garage together. Often they would accompany their father to races, where they would meet the world's most famous drivers and mechanics. Dale Jr. was still somewhat

BIG DALE

During Dale Jr.'s teen years, his dad was NASCAR's most dominant driver.

Season	Wins	Top 5s	Laps Led	Races Led	Ranking
1986	5	16	2,127*	26*	1
1987	11	21*	3,358*	27*	1
1988	3	13	1,808*	20**	3
1989	5	14**	2,735*	22	2
1990	9	18*	2,438*	22*	1
1991	4	14	1,125	20	1

* Led all Winston Cup drivers   ** Tied for Winston Cup lead

timid, while Kerry was fairly adventurous. It would not have surprised anyone who knew the boys if Kerry had become a top driver and Dale Jr. a top engine man.

"As a teenager, I didn't think Dale Jr. would be a racer," remembers Kerry. "He was not aggressive . . . and didn't take risks. Once I wrecked my Volkswagen on the farm, smashing the passenger door into a tree. Dale Jr. was with me and vowed he would never ride with me again."

Dale Jr.'s "driving resumé" was fairly thin to that point. He remembers the first time he ever commanded a real car, at the age of twelve. He and his dad were cruising down an empty highway when Dale told him to take the wheel. Dale Jr. became interested in racing radio-controlled cars for a while, then began tinkering with the go-kart that had once belonged to his grandfather. He mostly drove for fun—not because he was afraid of competing, but because he feared that losing would disappoint his father.

When Dale Jr. turned seventeen, he and Kerry went to the junkyard and picked out an old Monte Carlo. They brought it home and restored it, and all three kids took turns racing it in local events at the Concord Motorsports Park. When they weren't in the garage or at the track, they raced everything from horses to motorcycles on their father's farm.

Dale Sr. encouraged his children to explore their love of racing as long as they kept up with their schoolwork. He was especially tough on Dale Jr. "I always wanted him to get an education," he once said. "I always talked about that. My biggest regret is that I dropped out of school in ninth grade. My father told me it was a mistake. I just wouldn't listen. I wanted to make sure Dale Jr. didn't make the same mistake. It was a battle, but we got him through."

Pedal to the Metal

"It was like watching those old films of Ralph all over again."

— RACING VETERAN DON HAWK

Dale Jr. was nineteen when he began competing on NASCAR's Late Model circuit. The races took place on small ovals, in older cars. There were a few kids his age, but most of the drivers were in their twenties and thirties. For some, this was a stepping-stone to bigger and better things. For others, it was a way to fulfill a passion for racing. For everyone, it was a tough way to make a living. The expenses were high and the prize money was low. And at this level, there was little in the way of sponsorship or advertising money available.

Did You Know?

Everyone in racing called Dale Jr. "Little E" when he was growing up. When he became a racer in his own right, the nickname stuck!

Dale Jr. did well enough, winning three times in two years and finishing in the Top 5 in more than half the events he entered. But he still needed a regular job.

Dale Earnhardt, Inc., was a family business. Even little Taylor (Dale Jr.'s half sister) eventually went to work for the company.

Many fans assumed that Dale Jr. was getting a "free ride," that his dad was bankrolling his racing. But that was not the Earnhardt way. Every penny he put into racing came from his own hard work. "I suppose growing up with the Earnhardt name, I could have been a spoiled brat, but I wasn't," Dale Jr. recalls. "I don't think my dad would have put up with that anyway."

Dale Sr. now had his own company, Dale Earnhardt, Inc. (DEI). DEI built and sold cars, sponsored other NASCAR drivers, licensed memorabilia, and invested in many other areas. Kerry and Kelley went to work for DEI, and Dale Jr. was offered a job, too. It was not exactly an executive position. "You start at Dale Earnhardt, Inc., by sweeping floors and shoveling out the horse barn," he grimaces. "I was no exception."

Dale Sr. believed the rags-to-riches path built character and commitment in a young driver. He had come up this way, as had Ralph Earnhardt. Now the kids would, too. He offered Kerry, Kelley, and Dale Jr. all the encouragement they needed, but

A proud father stands with his sons Dale Jr. (left) and Kerry (right).
Many were surprised how serious Dale Jr. had become about racing.

rarely opened his wallet to finance their cars. He felt that if you couldn't afford to put a vehicle on the track every week, then you didn't want it badly enough. While Kerry and Kelley wavered under these rules, Dale Jr. went full speed ahead—eating, sleeping, and breathing stock-car racing.

Soon Dale Jr. was thinking of joining the Busch Series, which was just a notch below the Winston Cup circuit, where his dad competed. At the Busch level, he would be racing against the best up-and-coming drivers, as well as some of the wiliest NASCAR veterans. Was Dale Jr. aiming too high? His father certainly thought so. He kept reminding him that he had neither the cash nor the experience to make the jump. He still had to pay his dues. "All I heard from my dad was, 'You got to start at the bot-

"He can be as good as his dad."
RICHARD PETTY

tom, sweeping floors,'" Dale Jr.
recalls. "And I said, 'I'm going straight
to the driver's seat.' He'd laugh, but I
meant it."

In June 1996, at the age of twenty-
two, Dale Jr. scraped together enough
cash to get a car and crew to Myrtle
Beach, South Carolina, where he
entered the Busch Carolina Pride/Red
Dog 250. His qualifying run earned
him a spot in the third row of the
starting grid. During the race, he
drove well and finished 13th.

Although the result was nothing
to brag about, NASCAR veterans did
a double take when they watched
Dale Jr. wheel around the track. They
could tell from the way he drove that
he had plenty of Earnhardt in him—
a little bit of his dad and a lot of his
granddad. "It was scary how similar
they looked out on the race track,"
says Don Hawk, who was president
of DEI at the time.

Dale Sr. could not have been more proud of his son, although he still did not offer
to finance Dale Jr.'s Busch Series career. In fact, his next appearance at that level would
not come until 1997, when he managed to qualify for seven races. Dale Jr.'s best finish
was seventh in the Detroit Gasket 200 at the Michigan Speedway.

His most memorable moment came during the AC Delco 200 at North Carolina
Motor Speedway. Among the drivers in this race was his father. Several times they raced

A practice wreck early in Dale Jr.'s career convinced him to use the special head restraint pictured here. His father chose not to use it.

door-to-door and bumper-to-bumper, and "traded paint" on more than one occasion. After the race he asked his father what the deal was. "Didn't see a thing!" Dale Sr. smiled.

To the elder Earnhardt, being a racing dad meant letting your boy learn the sport's tough lessons firsthand—even if you end up being the driver who gives him the wake-up call. But he also knew when to step in and be fatherly. Once, Dale Jr. wrecked during practice. He walked away from the crash, but it really shook his confidence and made him think about quitting. Dale Sr. asked why his son would consider quitting. Dale Jr. admitted that when he messed up he felt that Dale Sr. had no confidence in him, and that made him want to stop.

Nothing could be farther from the truth, his father assured him.

Busch Leaguer

"He surprised a lot of people. I'd have never dreamed he'd be this good this fast."

— LARRY McREYNOLDS, *DEI CREW CHIEF*

Dale Sr. wanted his son to know he thought highly of him as a racer. But he did not want him to get too big for his britches, either. When he built a car for the 1998 Busch Series and asked Dale Jr. to test it for him, he did not come right out and tell him that DEI planned to hire him as its full-time driver. Normally, when an owner asks you to test a car, he is planning to put you behind the wheel once it is

Dale Sr. takes the checkered flag at Daytona in February 1998. It was the beginning of a big year for the Earnhardt family.

Dale Sr. hoists his first Daytona 500 trophy. Two months later his son won his first Busch Series race.

ready to start racing. But Dale Sr. wanted to mess with the kid a little before breaking the good news. Whenever the two were together, Dale Sr. always found a way to avoid the topic. And Dale Jr. was afraid to come right out and ask.

With the season-opening Busch Series races at Daytona looming on the horizon, there was still no word from dad. Dale Jr. began to worry. If he was not going to be driving for DEI, he needed to get his own car in shape for the 1998 season. If he was, why wasn't anyone saying anything? Worry turned to frustration and then to anger. But in the end, Dale Jr. realized this was just his father's way. "I wasn't sure I was the driver until the name decals came into the shop," he laughs. "I know he just wanted to teach me respect. He didn't want me to assume."

Although Dale Sr. had no qualms about giving his son a ride, some critics questioned whether he was rushing things. Would he have promoted another driver so quickly? Dale Sr. went on record saying that Dale Jr. had earned the opportunity and that anyone who believed otherwise had better look out—because Junior was going to have a big year. Dale Jr. never felt prouder.

Unfortunately, his pride did not help him at Daytona, where he flipped his car and finished 37th in the NAPA Auto Parts 300. Luckily, the family honor was preserved in the Daytona 500, which his father won for the first time. Victory in this race had eluded Dale Sr. for two decades. It was the crowning achievement of his career, and as he barreled down the straightaway toward the checkered flag, the hard-hearted "Intimidator" had tears streaming down his cheeks.

With the racing world's attention focused on Dale Sr., Dale Jr. went out and had himself quite a spring. In the weeks that followed, he captured two poles (the pole position—nearest the rail in the first row—is awarded to a race's fastest qualifier) and finished in the Top 5 four times. In early April, at the Texas Motor Speedway, he took his first Busch Series checkered flag in the Coca-Cola 300. Dale Jr. collected another victory in May, this one in the MBNA Platinum 200 at Dover Downs. He showed remarkable composure during this race when his car hit a slick patch of pavement on the way into the pits. The car spun 360 degrees before he regained control.

By the start of the summer, Dale Jr. was challenging for the Busch Series points lead. He had also established himself as the circuit's most popular driver. No longer was he regarded as a curiosity—now he was a star in his own right. This began to dawn on him when his pre-race autograph sessions began stretching past the 30-minute mark, with no end in sight. At an event in Hickory, North Carolina, Dale Jr. had to be "rescued" by his crew or he would have been late for the start. It was kind of cool to be that famous, but he was starting to see how success would change some of the small pleasures in his life. "I want all of the fans cheering me, and I want all of them to enjoy watching me race and to hope that I would win," he says. "But then again, I also miss the way things used to be."

With success came the realization that racing was no longer just a sport. It was now a

One of the coolest things about moving up the NASCAR ladder for Dale Jr. has been getting his own trading cards.

business. During the 1998 season, Dale Jr. signed an agreement that his dad's company would manage his business affairs. To his surprise, this deal did not include personal advice from Dale Sr. When it came to handling fame and juggling a schedule, he felt his son should figure things out for himself. "I'd welcome his input more," Dale admitted later that year.

Another thing Dale Jr. had to figure out for himself was just how aggressive he wanted to be on the track. He was not a clone of his dad in this respect, but he certainly was not afraid to make contact with other drivers. "I think that's what the sport needs," he says. "It's like watching boxing. You don't pay to see someone throw the jab all night. You want to see the knockout."

Busch Series Stats

Season	Starts	Victories	Top 5 Finishes	Ranking
1996	1	0	0	—
1997	8	0	0	47
1998	28	5	14	1
1999	31	6	18	1
2000	(Did Not Compete)			
2001	1	0	0	118
2002	3	2	2	60

Busch Series Achievements

Busch Series Champion . . . . 1998 & 1999

Dale Jr. finished out the 1998 season with five wins, scoring enough points in the remaining races to take the Busch Series championship. To become a full-time Winston Cup driver, he needed to have another solid year at the Busch Series level while entering a handful of Winston Cup events in 1999. If everything worked out, Dale Jr. would get a full-time ride in the "big leagues" by the 2000 season. Anheuser-Busch, the beer company that sponsored him, liked the plan, signing him to an eight-year contract worth a whopping $80 million.

Dale Jr. was ecstatic when he inked this deal. He was now set for life financially. What made him even more proud, however, was when his father told him DEI was building him his own garage. To him, this was the ultimate sign that he had made it as a race-car driver.

Did You Know?

Dale Jr. was put on probation by NASCAR in 1998 for running into Tony Stewart (right) during the Pike's Peak Hill Climb.

Dale Jr. gets some final words of advice before attempting to qualify for his first Winston Cup event in May 1999.

Busting Into the Big Time

chapter 5

"If you come from a champion litter you feel like you can do anything."

— DALE EARNHARDT JR.

ale Jr.'s Winston Cup debut would come at the Coca-Cola 600 in May 1999. In the meantime, he was back on the Busch circuit and not doing well at all. Defending his championship, living up to the big contract, worrying about the Winston Cup, fulfilling his new public appearance obligations—Dale Jr. was starting to feel as if he had bitten off more than he could chew. He failed to win a race all spring.

"It's funny. Before I actually became a race-car driver, I would watch Dad's races and would think that I knew exactly what he was doing and why he was doing it. Now that I'm out here and see what's going on, I realize I had no idea."

DALE EARNHARDT JR.

Dale Jr. cracks up veteran Mark Martin prior to a 1999 Winston Cup race. The older drivers got a big kick out of racing against "Little E."

"A lot of people say, 'You ought to be grateful, man. You've got the opportunity of a lifetime, blah, blah,' but they don't have to walk in these shoes," Dale Jr. says. "You can't eat, you can't sleep, you can't do anything without thinking about it—and dreading that life will never be like it was. A lot of advantages and rewards come with this, but you're so busy you don't have time to enjoy it. So sometimes you wonder, what good is it?"

As the Coca-Cola 600 neared, fans started to call it "E-Day." The pressure on Dale Jr. was intense. He breathed a little easier after qualifying eighth, and Dale Sr. tried to loosen him up with a little trackside humor, but he was too focused on the race to have

fun. When the green flag dropped at the Charlotte Motor Speedway, Dale Jr. roared off the start line but could not find his rhythm. He faded into the middle of the pack, never pushed the leaders, and finished 16th.

After the race, Dale Jr. felt more relieved than anything else. The first person he wanted to talk with was his dad. "He told me I did a good job, that I stayed clean and I stayed out of trouble," Dale Jr. remembers. "So I guess you could say after everything that went on, my debut got the ultimate stamp of approval."

As planned, Dale Jr. ran in four more Winston Cup races during 1999. His best finish was 10th place, but he was learning a lot. He had better luck on the Busch circuit, where he won at Dover Downs the week after his Winston Cup debut. Dale Jr. won races in each of the following two weeks, too—at the Textilease Medigue 300 and the Lycos 200—and finished off the summer with three more victories. Those wins, plus second-place finishes in the season's last three races, gave Dale Jr. the

Dale Jr. celebrates his second Busch Series championship in November 1999.

Dale Sr. hoists the winner's trophy at the 1999 IROC race in Michigan. The driver he beat to the finish line was Dale Jr.

points he needed to grab his second straight Busch championship.

In the end, Dale Jr.'s 1999 season was even more rewarding than his great 1998. The young man took a well-deserved breather that winter. He turned the basement of his house—a one-story structure on the Earnhardt family farm—into his own personal night-club, throwing parties almost every night. Dale Jr. would stumble into work bleary-eyed in the morning, under his father's disapproving glare. Dale Sr. never said a thing. He knew what lay ahead for his boy, and decided to let him enjoy this little bit of freedom while he could. As a Winston Cup driver in 2000, Dale Jr. would have more responsibilities than he ever imagined.

One Proud Papa

chapter 6

*"It's hard to believe your
kid can do something like that."*
— **DALE EARNHARDT SR.**

ale Earnhardt Jr., the two-time Busch champ, began the 2000 Winston Cup season as all rookies do: on the bottom of the pile. Although the other drivers respected his ability and the fans had begun to look past his famous last name, Dale Jr. still had to prove himself all over again. Eager to make an impression, he often tried to do too much, rather than trusting his car and crew to

"I love driving and signing autographs. But it's those other deals—banquets and dinners and meetings—that's the tough part. There's constantly somebody asking you to do this and do that, go here and go there. I knew that was part of it, but there was no breaking-in period. It was, wham, wide open from day one."
DALE EARNHARDT JR.

Winston Cup rookies Scott Pruett (left), Matt Kenseth (center), and Dale Jr. chat before the 2000 Daytona 500.

bring him home. The best finish he could muster in his first six races was a 10th, at the Las Vegas 400.

Dale Jr. did not become impatient. Though he had yet to make a breakthrough, he was getting used to his car, and his pit crew was starting to work like a well-oiled machine. As the Primestar 500 neared, he started to get a good feeling. This event was run at the Texas Motor Speedway, where he had always done well. Everything went smoothly in practice and qualifying, and when the race began, he had no trouble staying with the leaders. In the final stages, Dale Jr. opened up a six-second lead over the second-place car, driven by Jeff Burton, and cruised home to his first Winston Cup win. As difficult as the other races had been, this one was a breeze. "I didn't have to do

The Earnhardt File

DALE JR.'S FAVORITE...

Food . . . . Chicken

Snack . . . . Chips and Salsa

Actor . . . . Tom Hanks

Actress . . . . Cameron Diaz

Band . . . . Pearl Jam

Movie . . . . Days of Thunder

"The older I get, the more I can prove to others that I'm capable of making my own decisions, and prove to them they can trust my decisions."

a whole lot," marvels Dale Jr. "It was easy as pie."

No one in Texas was smiling bigger that day than Dale Earnhardt Sr. "He was pretty excited," his son remembers.

Dale Jr. was one of four rookies making a big splash in Winston Cup during the 2000 season. Joining him were Matt Kenseth, Stack Compton, and Scott Pruett. It had been a long time since NASCAR had seen so much talent breaking in at the same time. Some were saying this was the best group ever. The media immediately picked up on the "rivalry" between Dale Jr. and Kenseth. They were both young and fearless, and during their Busch Series days they often ran 1–2. It was Kenseth, in fact, who pushed Dale Jr. hardest in the point standings on his way to both of his championships. Would they continue their competition on the Winston Cup circuit?

In the first half of 2000, it seemed as if Dale Jr. would blow his old rival away. He won again at the Pontiac Excitement 400 in May at the Richmond International Speedway, then won NASCAR's annual All-Star race in Charlotte two weeks later. The Charlotte win was very impressive. With eight laps to go, Dale Jr. emerged from a pit stop in last place. Knowing the other drivers would soon pit, too, he floored it and maneuvered his way into the lead in time to take the checkered flag. There were

As this Ford giveaway shows, Matt Kenseth had the mighty automaker backing him during his rookie year.

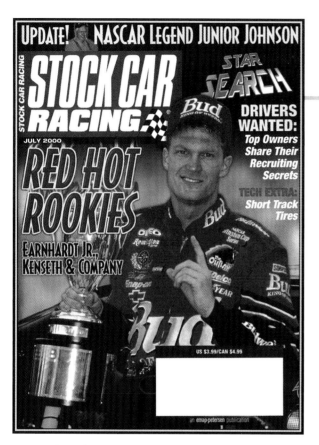

Although Dale Jr. finished second in the rookie balloting to Matt Kenseth, he won the battle of the magazine covers, appearing on more than a half-dozen in 2000.

170,000 fans in the stands, and they went crazy when Dale Jr. crossed the finish line. "This is the greatest," he said after the race. "Know why? Because it makes Daddy happy. That's number one, keeping Pops happy. For 20 years, I've tried to make things as hard as I could on him. Now we've turned it around, and I'm doing good for him."

The second half of the 2000 season was a different story. As often happens to fast-starting rookies, exhaustion set in and suddenly Dale Jr. and his car and his crew seemed out of sync. Even when things seemed to be going well, something would happen to ruin a race. With each disappointing finish, he searched for answers. Was he pushing too hard? Was he not pushing hard enough? Was his strategy flawed? These questions further eroded his confidence. Dale Jr. dropped out of the Top 10 in the Winston Cup standings and barely stayed in the Top 20.

Meanwhile, Kenseth was closing fast in the Rookie of the Year competition. What had earlier seemed to be a no-brainer turned into quite a tussle. In the second half, Kenseth showed excellent consistency, while Dale Jr. often failed to finish his races. This ultimately tipped the scales in Kenseth's favor.

Did You Know?

Dale Jr.'s first Winston Cup win—in only his twelfth start—was the second-earliest in history. Only Ron Bouchard (in 1981) captured his first victory sooner.

Still, it was one heck of a rookie year. The best part about it was that Dale Jr. and Dale

The two Dales get together before the Southern 500. They became great friends during the 2000 season.

Sr. were closer than ever. They were now much more than father and son—they were on-track competitors, off-track business partners, and best friends. It was one of the most heartwarming stories in sports.

Car owner Richard Childress, who knew Dale Sr. as well as anyone, put it best. "There's no question about it," he told a reporter. "Those two are as much buddies as they are father and son. They're hanging around off the track, and they're beating people on it."

Dark Day at Daytona

"He leaves a big, big void here that will be very hard to fill."

—HALL OF FAMER NED JARRETT

nlike other sports, stock-car racing kicks off its season with its biggest event. Since it started in 1959, the Daytona 500 has been NASCAR's Opening Day, All-Star Game, and Super Bowl all rolled into one. It not only sets the tone for the entire racing season, it also

"When I did good, he'd be there to share with me, and when I didn't do so good, he was there to help me, encourage me."

DALE EARNHARDT JR.

Dale Sr. (3) narrowly avoids Tony Stewart's car (20) as it goes airborne during the 2001 Daytona 500. His luck did not hold out.

creates tremendous anticipation all winter long. Indeed, the stock-car racing "off-season" is when a driver's hardest work starts. All the lessons from the previous year must be analyzed while setting a strategy for the coming campaign. A new car has to be constructed, sponsorship deals must be made, and mechanics and crew members must be hired and fired.

One of the major stories heading into the 2001 Daytona 500 was Dale Earnhardt Jr. His father knew everything there was to know about winning and losing this event, and now he was passing this wisdom on to his son. Most fans believed Dale Jr. had an

Dale Sr. (right) positions himself to block Ken Schrader.
This strategy may have cost him his life.

excellent chance of taking the checkered flag. Many insiders also had their eye on his DEI teammate, Michael Waltrip. Waltrip had refined skills, great instincts, and plenty of experience. He had been a Winston Cup regular since the mid-1980s, but had never won a major event. Many felt that this was because he always had second-rate cars and pit crews. Well, this year Waltrip had a top-notch car and the DEI team behind him. Dale Sr. believed his drivers might even finish 1–2 . . . if he didn't win it himself.

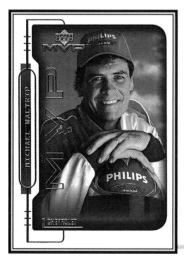

It was an exciting race with many lead changes. With less than 100 miles (161 km) to go, Dale Sr. looked like a genius. He and Waltrip and Dale Jr. were running out in front of everyone. On Lap 173 (of 200) the chances for a 1–2–3 finish looked pretty good. Just behind the Earnhardt cars, Robby Gordon, trying to pass Ward Burton, hit him from behind. Burton spun into Tony Stewart, whose car went airborne and ripped the hood off Bobby Labonte's car. After that, several other cars

Michael Waltrip's cards started drawing interest from collectors after he signed on with DEI—and demand skyrocketed after his win at Daytona.

To many, Dale Sr.'s crash at Daytona did not look serious. But those who saw his side window pop out knew he had hit the wall with tremendous force.

plowed into the wreckage. Luckily, no one was seriously hurt—although 19 cars were damaged and it took 15 minutes to clean up the track. When the race restarted, Ken Schrader and Rusty Wallace moved toward the front of the pack. Dale Sr. dropped behind Waltrip and his son, hoping to block out their pursuers. Schrader moved to pass Dale Sr. on the right, and Wallace dropped down low to pass him on the left.

What happened next is anyone's guess. Perhaps the "Intimidator" was trying to intimidate Schrader and Wallace at the same time. Maybe he was thinking too much about blocking and not enough about driving. Whatever Dale Sr. was doing, it caused

Dale Sr.'s Monte Carlo is covered by track workers as a stunned crowd looks on.

his Monte Carlo to shimmy and veer to the left, toward Wallace. He steered back to the right, but went too far, and Schrader's front end tapped him with enough force to rotate his car. Dale Sr. hit the wall on an angle at around 200 mph (322 kph), skidded for a moment, then came to rest on the infield. Up ahead, Waltrip pulled ahead of Dale Jr. to take the checkered flag. Neither driver knew their boss was in trouble.

Although the crash did not appear to be serious, it was obvious to the first people who reached Dale Sr. that something was wrong. He was not breathing, and blood was trickling from his ear. Doctors later determined that the force of the impact had snapped his neck at the base of his skull; he had died instantly. When Dale Jr. got the news, he was in shock. Seconds earlier he had been in the most exciting race of his life. Now his father was dead. When it all sank in he was inconsolable. "I had an awful nasty breakdown that day," he recalls. "I was screaming as loud as I could. I was in a room full of people, and it was like, 'Baaaaaah, I can't believe it.'"

Honor Thy Father

chapter 8

*"Every day I'm at the track,
I think about my dad."*

— DALE EARNHARDT JR.

he death of Dale Earnhardt Sr. cast a shadow over the entire season. He had become the sport's most popular personality and its most beloved driver. Fans had just gotten used to the idea that the Earnhardts would be putting on an unforgettable father-son performance for years to come. Then he was gone, just like that. Dale Jr. decided to keep racing, hoping that focusing on his work would ease the grief and the pain.

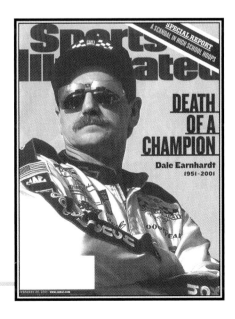

SPORTS ILLUSTRATED devoted its cover to Dale Sr. the week after his fatal accident.

As this picture shows, two weeks after Daytona the Earnhardt clan was still shattered by Dale Sr.'s death. Dale Jr. and his stepmother, Teresa, both suffered through long bouts of depression.

The following week, after the funeral and memorial service, Dale Jr. qualified for the KMart/Dura Lube 400. Climbing behind the wheel on race day was the hardest thing Dale Jr. ever had to do—especially after a moving pre-race ceremony honoring his father. In no shape to drive a car at 200 mph (322 kph), he crashed on the first lap.

Dale Jr. fell into a deep depression after that. He continued to compete, but his heart was no longer in it. Sometimes, it was tough just waking up in the morning. Instead of finding it easier to cope with his dad's death, it seemed to get harder and harder. Months passed, and nothing changed. July 4 loomed on the horizon—the day the Winston Cup would return to Daytona for the Pepsi 400. Dale Jr. dreaded the thought of competing on the same track that had taken his father's life; the mere thought sent chills down his spine.

Dale Jr. exults in victory after winning on the same track that took his father's life.

When he and his team arrived at the Daytona International Speedway, however, a different feeling came over him. Whenever he got behind the wheel, Dale Jr. swore he could sense his father's spirit. It was an uplifting experience, not a depressing one. On race day, he drove well for the first time in a long time, leading for more than 100 laps.

Fans kept their eyes glued to Dale Jr.'s number 8 car, wondering whether he could pull off a heart-wrenching victory. A 12-car pileup thinned out the field but left Dale Jr. in seventh place. Yet just when everyone was ready to write him off, he began to make up ground. He passed one car and then another. Soon he was within striking distance of the leaders.

The end of this race will be the subject of much debate, but the official results say Dale Earnhardt Jr. just blew everyone away. As he barreled into the lead, the other cars seemed to melt out of the way. "I have never been to a place where I was so dominant," he says.

When the checkered flag came down, there was not a dry eye in Daytona. What a perfect way to honor his father . . . and to shake off some of the demons that had been

Dale Jr. waves the Stars and Stripes after winning at Dover Downs in the first race held after the terror attacks of September 11, 2001.

tormenting him. Were his fellow drivers making room for him to pass out of respect for their fallen comrade? Or, as Dale Jr. claims, was his father there in the cockpit with him?

Released from months of anguish, Dale Jr. cut loose on his way to Victory Lane, turning doughnuts on the infield, then climbing out onto his hood and thrusting his arms into the air in celebration. The roar of the crowd was deafening, and it got even louder when the other drivers hopped out of their cars and mobbed him. "I want to dedicate this one to my dad," he told everyone. "This one is for him!"

The win at Daytona reenergized Dale Jr. He began to drive with more care and consistency. He won the MBNA/Cal Ripken Jr. 400 at Dover Downs, then drove to victory at Talladega a month later—the same race Dale Sr. had

Did You Know?

Dale Jr. says he sometimes receives eerie "visits" from his father—in his dreams. "He never has a starring role. He'll just be in the corner of some room."

won two years running. It felt good to keep the family winning streak alive. The victory also vaulted Dale Jr. into the Top 10 in the Winston Cup standings—one of his goals at the beginning of this upside-down year.

After the 2001 season, Dale Jr. finally had time to really think about his dad's life and death and the meaning of their relationship. Sometimes it made him incredibly sad, sometimes lonely, but also happy that they had become so close. In the end, Dale Jr. knew his papa was proud of him, and that was always what had mattered most.

LIKE FATHER, LIKE SON

After three full seasons on the Winston Cup circuit, Dale Jr.'s stats compare favorably to his father's. In Dale Sr.'s day, the difference between the top teams and the bottom teams was enormous. Today, the competition is fiercer than ever.

	Starts	Victories	Earnings
Dale Sr.	98	6	$1.5 million
Dale Jr.	11	7	$9.9 million

Dale Jr. (8) makes his move and takes the lead in the 2001 EA Sports 500. He won the race to crack the Top 10 in the rankings for the first time.

A New Man

chapter 9

*"Since my dad's accident,
everyone has been looking
to me to be more of a leader."*

— DALE EARNHARDT JR.

As the 2002 season got under way, everyone could see Dale Jr. was a different person. Although the magazine covers made much of his rock 'n' roll image, he was becoming more mature and serious. Like it or not, he was now the front man for the family business. "The main focus now," he says, "is to try to maintain and progress with the vision my father had with DEI."

Dale Jr. leans on car #3 prior to a 2002 race. He drove in several Busch Series events under his dad's old number.

Dale's work for his sponsors isn't all drudgery. Here he gets to hang out with Olympic skiing sensation Picabo Street.

At times, Dale Jr. was afraid he would not be up to the added responsibility. Some words of advice from Kyle Petty—whose son, Adam, also died in a crash—helped Dale Jr. focus on what is important. "He told me the best thing I can do is keep focused on driving the race car."

Dale Jr. did just that. He had his ups and downs in 2002—including a wreck that caused a nasty concussion—but through it all he remained focused on improving every aspect of his driving and earning the respect of the people whose opinion matters most now that his father is gone: the other drivers. In this area, Dale Jr. has made great strides. He even is starting to

Winston Cup *Stats*

Season	Starts	Victories	Top 5 Finishes	Ranking
1999	5	0	0	48
2000	34	2	4	16
2001	36	3	9	8
2002	36	2	11	11

remind people of Dale Sr. "I'll tell you, he's picked up right where his dad left off," says Jeff Gordon. "He's a smart driver and he knows when to drive his tail off."

What of his teen cult status and MTV image? Dale Jr. says he'll stick with whatever the fans like, as long as they realize that he's as serious about his craft as anyone on the stock-car circuit. "There's more to me professionally than just magazine covers, cool sponsors, and fun times," he says. "I want to win championships. There are all kinds of things that I want to do, and I know that I'll have to continue as a race car driver and be good at it."

He also knows that, whenever he needs a little something extra, somehow, some way, his father and grandfather will always be by his side.

Finally, there is the question that everyone wonders about, but nobody wants to ask: *Aren't you scared after what happened to your dad?*

Dale Jr. does not mind answering this question. He is the first to acknowledge that he is part of an extremely dangerous sport and that he is aware that every time he enters a race he could die. But scared? No way.

"If I quit driving race cars because of that," he says, "I wouldn't be living."

"His father would be proud of how he's handling things."

DRIVER JIMMY SPENCER

*Whenever Dale Jr. makes it to Victory Lane, he thinks about
how proud his father and grandfather would be.*

Index

Riverhead Free Library
330 Court Street
Riverhead, N.Y. 11901
727-3228

http://river.suffolk.lib.ny.us.

AUG   '03